making Classic Cakes

Traditional treats for family and friends

LORENZ BOOKS

This edition published by Lorenz Books
an imprint of
Anness Publishing Limited
Hermes House
88-89 Blackfriars Road
London SE1 8HA

This edition distributed in Canada by Raincoast Books
8680 Cambie Street, Vancouver, British Columbia V6P 6M9

A CIP catalogue record for this book is available from the British Library

ISBN 0 7548 0564 6

Publisher: Joanna Lorenz
Project Editor: Fiona Eaton
Designer: Lilian Lindblom
Contributers: Sue Maggs, Sarah Maxwell, Angela Nilson,
Janice Murfitt, Louise Pickford, Elizabeth Wolf-Cohen, Carole Clements
Photographers: Amanda Heywood, Edward Allwright, Karl Adamson,
Tim Hill, David Armstrong
Jacket Photographer: Amanda Heywood
Illustrator: Anna Koska

Also published as *30 Classic Cakes*

Printed and bound in Singapore

© Anness Publishing Limited 1996
Updated © 1999
1 3 5 7 9 10 8 6 4 2

CONTENTS

INTRODUCTION

Today cake making has rath. fallen out of fashion. Our busy life-styles, our attempts at healthy eating and calorie counting and sometimes our lack of baking skills have all contributed to the taste and enjoyment of home-baked goods being banished to just a delightful memory.

One misconception is that making a cake is difficult. This may well have been the case years ago when margarine was hard to cream, sugar may have been lumpy, ovens were unreliable and beating and whisking was laboriously done by hand. Nowadays it really is very easy to whip up a cake in next to no time. Ingredients are prepared, packaged and ready to use and there are mixers and food processors to whisk and blend to perfection in just a few seconds.

The recipes in this book are extremely straight-forward and quick to make. Each finished cake is fully illustrated, with some steps also shown for easy reference.

All of them have been tested and use easy-to-find ingredients and time-saving techniques, so even without any experience you will be able to turn out delicious and stunning cakes that cannot be bought.

There is something irresistible about a home-made cake. The shop-bought variety will never have the same smell, taste or uniqueness. Each time you make a cake it will turn out slightly differently and you can also choose to vary a cake by adding different ingredients or using an alternative shaped cake tin.

It is so much fun to make a cake – be it a simple Carrot Cake for weekend tea with the family to a special cake for Easter or Christmas. Not only will you have fun making the cake, but you will be amazed at how enthusiastically it is received.

So why not bring back those childhood memories of warm freshly baked cake for tea, turn the pages, choose your recipe and enjoy the many rewards that home baking can bring.

LEMON AND APRICOT CAKE

*This moreish cake is topped with a crunchy layer of flaked almonds
and pistachios, and is soaked in a tangy lemon syrup after baking
to keep it really moist.*

INGREDIENTS

SERVES 10–12

175 g/6 oz/¾ cup butter, softened
175 g/6 oz/1½ cups self-raising flour,
sifted
½ tsp baking powder
175 g/6 oz/¾ cup caster (superfine)
sugar
3 size 3 eggs, lightly beaten
finely grated rind of 1 lemon
175 g/6 oz/1½ cups ready-to-eat dried
apricots, finely chopped
75 g/3 oz/¾ cup ground almonds
40 g/1½ oz/¼ cup pistachios, chopped
50 g/2 oz/½ cup flaked almonds
15 g/½ oz/2 tbsp whole pistachios

FOR THE SYRUP
freshly squeezed juice of 1 lemon
3 tbsp caster (superfine) sugar

STORING
*This cake can be kept for up to 3 days
in an airtight container.*

1 Preheat the oven to 180°C/350°F/ Gas 4. Grease a 900 g/2 lb loaf tin, line the base and sides with greaseproof (wax) paper and grease the paper. Place the butter, flour and baking powder in a mixing bowl, then add the sugar, eggs and lemon rind. Beat for 1–2 minutes until smooth and glossy and then stir in the apricots, ground almonds and chopped pistachios.

3 To make the lemon syrup, put the lemon juice and sugar into a small saucepan and heat gently, stirring until the sugar has dissolved.

2 Spoon the mixture into the prepared tin and smooth the surface. Sprinkle with the flaked almonds and the whole pistachios. Bake in the centre of the oven for about 1¼ hours, or until a skewer inserted into the centre of the cake comes out clean. Check the cake after about 45 minutes and cover with a piece of foil when the top is nicely brown. Leave the cake to cool in the tin.

4 Spoon the syrup over the cake. When the cake is completely cold, turn it carefully out of the tin and peel off the lining paper.

MARBLED SPICE CAKE

This cake is baked in a fluted ring-shaped tin called a kugelhopf mould
(Bundt pan) from Germany and Austria to give it a pretty shape.

INGREDIENTS

SERVES 8–10
75 g/3 oz/6 tbsp butter, softened
115 g/4 oz/½ cup caster (superfine)
sugar
2 size 3 eggs, lightly beaten
a few drops of vanilla essence (extract)
115 g/4 oz/1 cup plain (all-purpose)
flour
1½ tsp baking powder
3 tbsp milk
3 tbsp black treacle (molasses)
1 tsp mixed spice (apple pie spice)
½ tsp ground ginger
175 g/6 oz/1½ cups icing
(confectioner's) sugar, sifted, to
decorate

STORING
This cake can be kept for up to 2 days
in an airtight container.

COOK'S TIP
If you do not have a kugelhopf
mould (Bundt pan) or a ring-shaped
cake tin, use a 20 cm/8 inch round
cake tin.

1 Preheat the oven to 180°C/350°F/
Gas 4. Grease and flour a 900 g/
2 lb kugelhopf mould (Bundt pan) or
deep ring-shaped cake tin. Cream the
butter and sugar together in a bowl
until light and fluffy. Beat in the egg
and vanilla essence (extract). Sift
together the flour and baking
powder, then fold into the mixture,
alternating with the milk, until evenly
combined. Spoon about one-third of
the mixture into a small bowl and
stir in the black treacle (molasses)
and spices.

3 Bake in the centre of the oven
for about 50 minutes or until a
skewer inserted into the centre comes
out clean. Leave in the tin for about
10 minutes before turning out on to
a wire rack to cool.

2 Drop alternating spoonfuls of
the light and dark mixtures into
the tin. Run a knife or skewer
through them to give a marbled
effect to the cake.

4 To decorate, stir enough warm
water into the icing
(confectioner's) sugar to make a
smooth icing. Spoon quickly over the
cake. Allow to set before serving.

JEWEL CAKE

This pretty tea-time cake is excellent served as an afternoon treat with tea or coffee.

INGREDIENTS

SERVES 10–15

115 g/4 oz/¾ cup mixed coloured glacé (candied) cherries, halved, washed and dried
50 g/2 oz/¼ cup stem (preserved) ginger in syrup, drained, washed, dried and chopped
50 g/2 oz/⅓ cup chopped mixed (candied) peel
115 g/4 oz/1 cup self-raising flour
75 g/3 oz/¾ cup plain (all-purpose) flour
25 g/1 oz/3 tbsp cornflour (cornstarch)
175 g/6 oz/¾ cup butter
175 g/6 oz/¾ cup caster (superfine) sugar
3 size 3 eggs
finely grated rind of 1 orange

TO DECORATE

175 g/6 oz/1½ cups icing (confectioner's) sugar, sifted
2–3 tbsp freshly squeezed orange juice
50 g/2 oz/¼ cup mixed coloured glacé (candied) cherries, chopped
25 g/1 oz/2½ tbsp chopped mixed (candied) peel

STORING

This cake can be kept for up to 2 days in an airtight container.

1 Preheat the oven to 180°C/350°F/ Gas 4. Grease a 900 g/2 lb loaf tin, line the base and sides with greaseproof (wax) paper and grease the paper. Place the cherries, ginger and peel in a plastic bag with 25 g/ 1 oz/¼ cup of the self-raising flour and shake to coat evenly. Sift the remaining flours and cornflour (cornstarch) into a small bowl.

2 Place the butter and sugar in a mixing bowl and beat until light and fluffy. Beat in the eggs, one at a time, until evenly blended. Fold in the flours with the orange rind, then stir in the fruit. Transfer the cake mixture to the prepared tin and bake in the centre of the oven for about 1¼ hours, or until a skewer inserted into the centre of the cake comes out clean. Leave the cake in the tin for 5 minutes, then turn out to cool.

3 To decorate the cake, place the icing (confectioner's) sugar in a mixing bowl. Stir in the orange juice and mix until smooth. Drizzle the icing over the cake. Mix together the chopped cherries and peel in a small bowl, then use to decorate the cake. Allow the icing to set before serving.

SUMMER STRAWBERRY SHORTCAKE

A summer-time treat. Serve with a cool glass of pink sparkling wine
for a truly refreshing dessert.

INGREDIENTS

SERVES 6–8
225 g/8 oz/2 cups plain (all-purpose)
flour
1 tbsp baking powder
½ tsp salt
50 g/2 oz/4 tbsp caster (superfine)
sugar
50 g/2 oz/4 tbsp butter, softened
150 ml/¼ pint/⅔ cup milk
300 ml/½ pint/1¼ cups double (heavy)
cream
450 g/1 lb fresh strawberries, halved
and hulled

STORING
This cake is not suitable for storing.

1 Preheat the oven to 220°C/
425°F/Gas 7. Grease a baking
(cookie) sheet, line with greaseproof
(wax) paper and grease the paper.
Sift the flour, baking powder and salt
together into a large mixing bowl.
Stir in the sugar, cut in the butter
and rub into the flour mixture until
it resembles coarse breadcrumbs. Stir
in just enough milk to make a soft,
pliable dough.

2 Place the dough on a lightly
floured surface and pat into a
30 x 15 cm/12 x 6 inch rectangle.
Cut out two 15 cm/6 inch rounds.
With the back of a knife, mark one
round into eight portions. Place the
rounds on the baking sheet.

3 Bake in the centre of the oven
for 10–15 minutes or until
slightly risen and golden. Leave the
shortcake on the baking sheet for
about 5 minutes, then transfer to a
wire rack, peel off the lining paper
and leave to cool completely.

4 Place the cream in a mixing
bowl and whip until it holds soft
peaks. Place the unmarked shortcake
on a serving plate and spread or pipe
with half of the cream. Top with
two-thirds of the strawberries, then
the other shortcake. Use the
remaining cream and strawberries to
decorate the top layer. Chill for at
least 30 minutes before serving.

CARROT CAKE

So easy to make, this is a wonderfully moist and tasty cake, enriched with grated carrots and vegetable oil – a classic "all-in-one" cake.

INGREDIENTS

SERVES 8

225 g/8 oz/1 cup caster (superfine) sugar
3 size 3 eggs
200 ml/7 fl oz/scant 1 cup vegetable oil
grated rind and juice of 1 orange
225 g/8 oz/2 cups self-raising wholemeal (whole wheat) flour
1 tsp ground cinnamon
½ tsp grated nutmeg
½ tsp salt
350 g/12 oz/2½ cups grated carrot, squeezed dry
115 g/4 oz/1 cup walnuts, ground
225 g/8 oz/1 cup cream cheese
2 tbsp clear honey
1 tbsp orange juice

TO DECORATE

50 g/2 oz/¼ cup ready-made marzipan
orange food colouring
angelica
2 walnut halves (optional)

STORING
This cake keeps for up to 1 week in an airtight container.

1 Preheat the oven to 180°C/350°F/ Gas 4. Lightly grease a deep 20 cm/8 inch round cake tin, line with greaseproof (wax) paper and grease the paper. Beat the sugar, eggs, oil, orange rind and juice together until light and frothy. Sift in the flour, spices and salt and beat for 1 minute. Stir in the carrots and nuts and transfer to the tin. Bake for 1½– 1¾ hours or until a skewer inserted into the centre comes out clean. Leave in the tin for 10 minutes before turning out on to a wire rack.

3 Tint the marzipan with the food colouring to resemble the colour of carrots.

2 To make the icing, beat the cheese, honey and 1 tbsp orange juice together until smooth. Chill for 30 minutes until firm.

4 Break off small pieces and roll between your palms to form carrot shapes. Using a small knife, press marks around the sides and stick a small piece of angelica in the top of each one for the stalk. Spread the icing over the top of the cooled cake. Arrange the carrots in the centre of the cake and decorate with the walnut halves, if using.

Banana Coconut Cake

Slightly over-ripe bananas are best for this perfect coffee morning cake.

Ingredients

Serves 8–10
75 g/3 oz/1½ cups desiccated (shredded) coconut
115 g/4 oz/½ cup butter, softened
115 g/4 oz/½ cup caster (superfine) sugar
2 size 3 eggs
115 g/4 oz/1 cup self-raising flour
50 g/2 oz/½ cup plain (all-purpose) flour
1 tsp bicarbonate of soda (baking soda)
120 ml/4 fl oz/½ cup milk
2 large bananas, peeled and mashed

For the Topping
25 g/1 oz/2 tbsp butter
2 tbsp clear honey
115 g/4 oz/2 cups desiccated (shredded) coconut

Storing
This cake will keep for up to 2 days in an airtight container.

3 Bake in the centre of the oven for about 1 hour, or until a skewer inserted into the centre of the cake comes out clean. Leave the cake in the tin for about 5 minutes, then turn out on to a wire rack, peel off the lining paper and leave to cool completely.

1 Preheat the oven to 190°C/375°F/ Gas 5. Grease a deep 18 cm/ 7 inch square cake tin, line the base and sides with greaseproof (wax) paper and then grease the paper. Spread the coconut out on a baking (cookie) sheet and place under a hot grill (broiler) for about 5 minutes, stirring and turning the coconut until evenly toasted.

2 Place the softened butter and caster (superfine) sugar in a mixing bowl and beat until they are smooth and creamy. Beat in the eggs, one at a time. Sift together the self-raising and plain (all-purpose) flours and bicarbonate of soda (baking soda), then sift half of this mixture into the butter and egg mixture and stir to mix. Mix together the milk and mashed banana in a small bowl, then add half to the egg mixture. Beat well to combine. Add the remaining flour and toasted coconut together with the remaining banana mixture. Stir to mix. Spoon the mixture into the prepared cake tin and smooth the surface with a wet knife.

4 To make the topping, place the butter and honey in a small saucepan and heat gently until melted. Stir in the desiccated (shredded) coconut and cook, stirring constantly, for about 5 minutes or until lightly browned. Remove from the heat and allow to cool slightly. Spoon the topping over the top of the cake and allow to cool completely before serving.

CRUNCHY-TOPPED MADEIRA CAKE

Traditionally served with a glass of Madeira wine in Victorian England,
this light sponge still makes a perfect tea-time treat.

INGREDIENTS

SERVES 8–10
200 g/7 oz/scant 1 cup butter, softened
finely grated rind of 1 lemon
150 g/5 oz/¾ cup caster (superfine)
sugar
3 size 3 eggs
75 g/3 oz/¾ cup plain (all-purpose)
flour, sifted
150 g/5 oz/1¼ cups self-raising flour,
sifted

FOR THE TOPPING
3 tbsp clear honey
115 g/4 oz/¾ cup plus 2 tbsp chopped
mixed (candied) peel
50 g/2 oz/½ cup flaked almonds

STORING
This cake can be kept for up to 3 days
in an airtight container.

1 Preheat the oven to 180°C/350°F/ Gas 4. Grease a 450 g/1 lb loaf tin, line the base and sides with greaseproof (wax) paper and grease the paper. Place the butter, lemon rind and sugar in a mixing bowl and beat until light and fluffy. Beat in the eggs, one at a time, beating well after each addition until evenly blended.

2 Sift together the flours, then stir into the egg mixture. Transfer the cake mixture to the prepared tin and smooth the surface. Bake in the centre of the oven for 45–50 minutes or until a skewer inserted into the centre of the cake comes out clean. Leave the cake in the tin for about 5 minutes. Turn out on to a wire rack, peel off the lining paper and leave to cool completely.

3 To make the topping, place the honey, chopped mixed (candied) peel and flaked almonds in a small saucepan and heat gently until the honey melts. Remove from the heat and stir briefly to coat the peel and almonds, then spread over the top of the cake. Allow to cool completely before serving.

GORGEOUS CHOCOLATE CAKE

This recipe will definitely make you famous. Make sure you serve it with
paper and pen, as everyone will want to take down the recipe.

INGREDIENTS

SERVES 8–10
175 g/6 oz/¾ cup butter, softened
115 g/4 oz/½ cup caster (superfine)
sugar
250 g/9 oz plain (semi-sweet)
chocolate, melted
200 g/7 oz/2 cups ground almonds
4 size 3 eggs, separated
115 g/4 oz white chocolate, melted,
to decorate

STORING
This cake can be kept for up to 4 days
in an airtight container.

COOK'S TIP
To make the chocolate leaves, wash
5 or 6 rose leaves well and dry on
kitchen paper (paper towels). Brush
the underside of each leaf with the
melted white chocolate. Place the
leaves chocolate-side up on non-stick
baking paper (baking parchment),
and leave to set in a cool place. Peel
the leaf from the chocolate and use
as required.

1 Preheat the oven to 180°C/350°F/
Gas 4. Grease a deep 21 cm/
8 inch springform cake tin, then line
the base with greaseproof (wax)
paper and grease the paper. Place
115 g/4 oz/½ cup of the butter and
all the sugar in a mixing bowl and
beat until light and fluffy. Add two-
thirds of the plain (semi-sweet)
chocolate, the ground almonds and
the egg yolks and beat until they are
evenly blended.

2 Whisk the egg whites in another
clean, dry bowl until stiff. Fold
them into the chocolate mixture, then
transfer to the prepared tin and
smooth the surface. Bake for 50–55
minutes or until a skewer inserted
into the centre of the cake comes out
clean. Leave the cake in the tin for
about 5 minutes, then turn out on to
a wire rack, peel off the lining paper
and leave to cool completely.

3 Place the remaining butter and
remaining melted plain chocolate
in a saucepan. Heat very gently,
stirring constantly, until melted. Pour
over the cake, allowing the topping
to coat the sides. Leave to set for at
least an hour. To decorate, fill a
piping bag with the melted white
chocolate and snip the end. Drizzle
all around the edges to make a
double border. Use any remaining
chocolate to make leaves.

APPLE CRUMBLE CAKE

In the autumn use windfall apples. Served warm with double (heavy) cream
or custard this cake doubles as a marvellous dessert.

INGREDIENTS

SERVES 8–10
75 g/3 oz/¾ cup self-raising flour
½ tsp ground cinnamon
40 g/1½ oz/3 tbsp butter
25 g/1 oz/2 tbsp caster (superfine)
sugar

FOR THE BASE
50 g/2 oz/4 tbsp butter, softened
75 g/3 oz/6 tbsp caster (superfine)
sugar
1 size 3 egg, beaten
115 g/4 oz/1 cup self-raising flour,
sifted
cooking apples, peeled,
cored and sliced
50 g/2 oz/½ cup sultanas
(golden raisins)

TO DECORATE
1 red eating apple, cored, thinly sliced
and tossed in lemon juice
2 tbsp caster (superfine) sugar
pinch of ground cinnamon

1 Preheat the oven to 180°C/350°F/ Gas 4. Grease a deep 18 cm/ 7 inch springform tin, line with greaseproof (wax) paper and grease the paper. To make the topping, sift the flour and cinnamon into a mixing bowl. Rub the butter into the flour until it resembles breadcrumbs, then stir in the sugar. Set aside.

2 To make the base, put the butter, sugar, egg and flour into a bowl and beat for 1–2 minutes until smooth. Spoon into the prepared tin. Mix together the apple slices and sultanas (golden raisins) and spread them over the top.

3 Sprinkle with the topping. Bake in the centre of the oven for about 1 hour. Cool in the tin for 10 minutes before turning out on to a wire rack and peeling off the lining paper. Serve warm or cool, decorated with slices of red eating apple and with the sugar and cinnamon sprinkled over.

UPSIDE-DOWN PEAR & GINGER CAKE

A light spicy sponge topped with glossy baked fruit and ginger. This is also good served warm for pudding.

INGREDIENTS

SERVES 6–8

900 g/2 lb can pear halves, drained
8 tbsp finely chopped stem (preserved) ginger
8 tbsp ginger syrup from the jar
175 g/6 oz/1½ cups self-raising flour
½ tsp baking powder
1 tsp ground ginger
175 g/6 oz/¾ cup soft light brown sugar
175 g/6 oz/¾ cup butter, softened
3 size 3 eggs, lightly beaten

1 Preheat the oven to 180°C/350°F/ Gas 4. Grease a deep 20 cm/ 8 inch round cake tin, line with greaseproof (wax) paper and grease the paper. Fill the pears with half the chopped ginger. Arrange the pears, flat sides down, in the tin. Spoon half the ginger syrup over the top.

2 Sift the flour, baking powder and ground ginger into a mixing bowl. Stir in the soft brown sugar and butter, then add the eggs and beat together for 1–2 minutes until light and creamy. Spoon the mixture into the tin and smooth the surface.

3 Bake in the centre of the oven for 50 minutes, or until a skewer inserted in the centre of the cake comes out clean. Leave the cake in the tin for 5 minutes. Then turn out and leave to cool. Add the reserved chopped ginger to the pear halves and drizzle over the remaining ginger syrup.

SOUR CREAM CRUMBLE CAKE

*A deliciously moist sponge, filled and topped with a spicy crumble of
walnuts, brown sugar and cinnamon. For a special treat serve with
whipped cream or Greek-style yogurt.*

INGREDIENTS

SERVES 12–14
*115 g/4 oz/½ cup butter,
at room temperature*
*125 g/4½ oz/¾ cup caster (superfine)
sugar*
3 size 3 eggs, at room temperature
*215 g/7½ oz/scant 2 cups plain
(all-purpose) flour*
*1 tsp bicarbonate of soda
(baking soda)*
1 tsp baking powder
250 ml/8 fl oz/1 cup sour cream

FOR THE TOPPING
225 g/8 oz/1½ cups dark brown sugar
2 tsp ground cinnamon
*115 g/4 oz/1 cup walnuts,
finely chopped*
*50 g/2 oz/¼ cup cold butter,
cut into pieces*

STORING
*This cake can be kept for up to 3 days
in an airtight container.*

1 Preheat the oven to 180°C/350°F/
Gas 4. Grease a deep 23 cm/
9 inch square cake tin then line the
base with greaseproof (wax) paper
and grease the paper. For the topping,
place the brown sugar, cinnamon and
walnuts in a bowl. Rub together with
your fingertips, then rub in the butter
and continue working until the
mixture resembles breadcrumbs.

2 To make the cake, cream the
butter until soft. Add the sugar
and continue beating until the
mixture is light and fluffy. Add the
eggs, one at a time, beating well after
each addition.

3 In another bowl, sift the flour,
bicarbonate of soda (baking
soda) and baking powder together
three times. Fold the dry ingredients
into the butter mixture in 3 batches,
alternating with the sour cream. Fold
in each addition until well-blended.

4 Pour half of the batter into the
prepared tin and sprinkle over
half of the walnut crumb topping
mixture. Pour the remaining batter
on top and sprinkle over the
remaining walnut crumb mixture.
Bake until brown, 60–70 minutes.
Let the cake stand for 5 minutes,
then turn it out to cool on a rack.

PEAR AND CARDAMOM SPICE CAKE

Fresh pear and cardamom – a classic combination of flavours – are used together in this moist fruit and nut cake to provide a delicious, mouthwatering tea-time treat.

INGREDIENTS

Serves 8–12
115 g/4 oz/½ cup butter
115 g/4 oz/½ cup caster (superfine) sugar
2 size 3 eggs, lightly beaten
225 g/8 oz/2 cups plain (all-purpose) flour
1 tbsp baking powder
2 tbsp milk
crushed seeds from 2 cardamom pods
50 g/2 oz/½ cup walnuts, chopped
1 tbsp poppy seeds
575 g/1¼ lb dessert pears, peeled, cored and thinly sliced

FOR THE TOPPING
3 walnut halves
reserved pear slices
3 tbsp clear honey

STORING
This cake can be kept in an airtight container for several days.

1 Preheat the oven to 180°C/350°F/ Gas 4. Lightly grease a deep 20 cm/8 inch round loose-based cake tin, line the base with greaseproof (wax) paper and grease the paper. Cream the butter and caster (superfine) sugar together until the mixture is light and fluffy. Gradually beat in the eggs, a little at a time, until evenly blended. Sift the plain (all-purpose) flour and baking powder together, and then fold in gradually along with the milk.

3 Place the 3 walnut halves in the centre of the cake mixture, and fan the reserved pear slices around the walnuts, covering the cake mixture. Bake for 1¼–1½ hours, or until a skewer inserted into the centre comes out clean.

2 Stir in the cardamom seeds, chopped nuts and poppy seeds. Reserve one-third of the pear slices; chop the rest. Fold the chopped pears into the creamed mixture. Transfer to the prepared tin. Smooth the surface, making a small dip in the centre.

4 Remove the cake from the oven and brush with the clear honey. Cool in the tin for 20 minutes, and then transfer to a wire rack and allow to cool completely.

DUNDEE CAKE

*This is the perfect fruit cake for those who prefer a lighter-style cake. It has
a wonderful fruit and nut flavour and a light, slightly crumbly texture.*

INGREDIENTS

SERVES 16–20
175 g/6 oz/¾ cup butter
176 g/6 oz/scant ¾ cup light soft
brown sugar
3 size 3 eggs
225 g/8 oz/2 cups plain (all-purpose)
flour
2 tsp baking powder
1 tsp ground cinnamon
½ tsp ground cloves
¼ tsp ground nutmeg
225 g/8 oz/1¼ cups sultanas
(golden raisins)
175 g/6 oz/1 cup raisins
175 g/6 oz/1 cup glacé (candied)
cherries, halved
115 g/4 oz/¾ cup chopped mixed
(candied) peel
50 g/2 oz/¾ cup blanched almonds,
chopped
grated rind 1 lemon
2 tbsp brandy

FOR THE TOPPING
75–115 g/3–4 oz/¾–1cup whole
blanched almonds

STORING
*All fruit cakes improve in flavour if
left in a cool place for up to three
months. Wrap the cake in a double
layer of foil.*

2 Spoon into the prepared tin,
smooth the surface, making a
small dip in the centre.

1 Preheat the oven to 160°C/325°F/
Gas 3. Grease a deep 20 cm/
8 inch round cake tin, line the base
and sides with greaseproof (wax)
paper and then grease the paper.
Cream the butter and sugar together
until light and fluffy. Add the eggs,
one at a time, beating well after each
addition. Sift the flour, baking
powder and spices together and fold
into the creamed mixture alternately
with the remaining ingredients, until
evenly incorporated.

3 Decorate the top of the cake
mixture by pressing the almonds
in decreasing circles over the entire
surface. Bake for 2–2¼ hours, or
until a skewer inserted in the centre
comes out clean. Remove from the
oven, cool in the tin for 30 minutes,
and then transfer to a wire rack to
cool completely.

ALMOND AND APRICOT CAKE

Although canned apricots can be used in this recipe, nothing quite beats using the fresh fruit in season. Choose sweet-smelling, ripe fruit for this delicious cake.

INGREDIENTS

SERVES 6–8
4–5 tbsp fine dry white breadcrumbs
225 g/8 oz/1 cup butter, softened
225 g/8 oz/1 cup caster (superfine)
sugar
4 size 3 eggs
175 g/6 oz/1½ cups self-raising flour,
sifted
1–2 tbsp milk
115 g/4 oz/1 cup ground almonds
a few drops of almond essence
(extract)
450 g/1 lb fresh apricots, stoned
(pitted) and halved
sifted caster (superfine) sugar, to
decorate

STORING
This cake can be kept for up to 3 days
in an airtight container.

1 Preheat the oven to 180°C/350°F/ Gas 4. Grease a 23 cm/9 inch round cake tin, line the base with greaseproof (wax) paper and grease the paper. Sprinkle the breadcrumbs into the prepared cake tin and tap them around the tin to coat the base and sides evenly.

2 Place the butter and sugar in a mixing bowl and beat until light and fluffy. Beat in the eggs, one at a time, then fold in the flour, together with the milk, ground almonds and almond essence (extract).

3 Spoon half of the cake mixture into the prepared tin and smooth the surface. Arrange half of the apricots over the top, then spoon over the remaining cake mixture. Finish with the other half of the apricots. Bake the cake in the centre of the oven for 30–35 minutes, or until a skewer inserted into the centre of the cake comes out clean. Turn the cake out on to a wire rack, peel off the lining paper and sprinkle over the sifted caster (superfine) sugar. Serve warm or leave to cool.

MISSISSIPPI MUD CAKE

This dark cocoa-based chocolate cake is meant to be reminiscent
of the cocoa-black shores of the Mississippi River.

INGREDIENTS

SERVES 8–10
unsweetened cocoa powder
275 g/10 oz/2½ cups plain
(all-purpose) flour
1 tsp baking powder
150 g/5 oz unsweetened chocolate
225 g/8 oz/1 cup unsalted (sweet)
butter
300 ml/½ pint/1¼ cups strong coffee
pinch of salt
400 g/14 oz/2 cups granulated sugar
60 ml/2 fl oz/¼ cup whisky
2 size 3 eggs, lightly beaten
2 tsp vanilla essence (extract)
115 g/4 oz/1 cup sweetened desiccated
(shredded) coconut

FOR THE FILLING
250 ml/8 fl oz/1 cup evaporated milk
115 g/4 oz/⅔ cup light brown sugar
115 g/4 oz/½ cup unsalted (sweet)
butter
75 g/3 oz plain (semi-sweet) chocolate
3 egg yolks, lightly beaten
1 tsp vanilla essence (extract)
225 g/8 oz/2 cups pecan nuts, chopped
70 g/2½ oz/1 cup miniature
marshmallows

FOR THE TOPPING
350 ml/12 fl oz/1½ cups whipping or
double (heavy) cream
1 tsp vanilla essence (extract)
coconut ruffles (see step 4)

1 Preheat the oven to 180°C/350°F/ Gas 4. Grease 2 x 23 cm/9 inch cake tins and dust the bases and sides with cocoa powder. In a bowl sift the flour and baking powder. In a saucepan over a low heat, melt the chocolate, butter, coffee, salt and sugar, stirring occasionally until the sugar has dissolved. Stir in the whisky. Pour the chocolate mixture into a bowl and cool. Beat in the eggs and vanilla. Stir in the flour and coconut. Pour into the prepared tins, then bake for 25–30 minutes or until a skewer inserted in the centre comes out clean. Cool in the tins on a wire rack for 10 minutes, then turn out on to the wire rack and leave to cool completely.

2 For the filling, put the evaporated milk, sugar, butter, chocolate, egg yolks and vanilla in a saucepan. Cook over a medium heat, stirring frequently for 8–10 minutes until the chocolate has melted and the mixture coats the back of a wooden spoon; do not boil or the mixture will curdle. Remove from the heat and add the nuts and marshmallows, stirring until melted. Chill until thick enough to spread, stirring occasionally.

3 Slice both cake layers in half horizontally. Spread each of the bottom cake layers with half the chocolate nut filling and top with the other halves. Whip the cream and the vanilla until it holds firm peaks. Place one filled cake on a plate and spread with half the whipped cream. Top with the second filled cake and spread with the remaining cream.

4 To make the coconut ruffles, puncture the eyes of a coconut with a nail and hammer. Drain, then crack the coconut open using the hammer. Remove the flesh from the shell using a strong, blunt-bladed knife. Rinse in cold water. Using a potato peeler, shave along the curved edge of a coconut piece to give thin wide curls with a brown edge. Use to decorate the cake.

CHILLED GRAPE CHEESECAKE

An attractive and unusual topping decorates this classic chilled cheesecake.
Use green grapes and white grape juice if wished, for an equally attractive cheesecake.

INGREDIENTS

SERVES 12

175 g/6 oz/2 cups crushed gingernuts
(ginger cookies)
50 g/2 oz/¼ cup unsalted (sweet)
butter, melted
350 g/12 oz/1½ cups cream cheese
200 g/7 oz/1 scant cup fromage frais
6 tbsp clear honey
2 size 3 eggs, separated
1 tsp grated lemon rind
1 tbsp lemon juice
4 tbsp Muscat de Beaumes
de Venise (or other sweet white
dessert wine)
1 tbsp powdered gelatine

FOR THE TOPPING
115 g/4 oz red or green seedless
grapes, halved
small piece angelica
2 tbsp Muscat de Beaumes
de Venise (or other sweet white
dessert wine)
1½ tsp powdered gelatine
300 ml/½ pt/1¼ cups red or white
grape juice

STORING
*Place in an airtight container and keep
in the refrigerator for up to 3 days.*

1 Grease a 23 cm/9 inch round springform tin and line the sides with non-stick baking paper (baking parchment). Combine the gingernuts (ginger cookies) with the butter until well mixed. Press into the base of the prepared tin. Smooth the surface with a metal spoon and chill for 20 minutes. To prepare the cake mixture, beat the cheese, fromage frais, honey, egg yolks, lemon rind and juice in a bowl, until smooth and creamy.

3 When the cheesecake is just setting, remove from the refridgerator and arrange the grapes over the top, in the shape of a bunch of grapes, and make a stalk from the angelica. Chill until completely set. For the topping, heat the 2 tbsp of wine and the gelatine together as before, until dissolved. Pour in the grape juice and leave to go cold.

2 Heat the 4 tbsp of wine and the gelatine together in a small pan, over a low heat, until the gelatine dissolves. Remove from the heat, stir in a little of the creamed mixture, and pour back into the remaining creamed mixture mixing until combined. Whisk the egg whites until stiff and fold thoroughly into the creamed mixture. Pour over the chilled biscuit (cookie) base and chill.

4 Using a small paintbrush, carefully dampen the edges of the lined tin, directly above the set cheesecake. Carefully pour over the cooled grape juice to cover the grapes and chill until set. Just before serving, remove the tin from the side of the cheesecake and carefully peel away the lining paper using a palette knife (metal spatula) to help.

Raspberry-hazelnut Meringue Cake

Crisp layers of hazelnut meringue, whipped cream and fresh raspberries make this a wonderful dessert to serve at a summer dinner party.

Ingredients

Serves 8
150 g/5 oz/1¼ cups shelled hazelnuts
4 egg whites
¾ tsp salt
200 g/7 oz/1 cup caster (superfine) sugar
½ tsp vanilla essence (extract)

For the Filling
300 ml/½ pint/1¼ cups whipping cream
700 g/1½ lb/4 cups raspberries

Storing
This cake is not suitable for storing.

1 Preheat the oven to 180°C/350°F/ Gas 4. Grease two 20 cm/8 inch sandwich tins and line the bases with greaseproof (wax) paper, and grease the paper. Spread the hazelnuts on a baking (cookie) sheet and bake until lightly toasted, about 8 minutes. Leave the nuts to cool slightly.

2 Rub the hazelnuts in a clean dish towel to remove the skins. Grind the nuts in a food processor or coffee grinder until they are the consistency of coarse sand. Reduce the oven to 150°C/300°F/Gas 2.

3 With an electric mixer, beat the egg whites and salt until they hold stiff peaks. Beat in 2 tbsp of the sugar, then fold in the remaining sugar, a few tablespoons at a time. Fold in the vanilla essence (extract) and the ground hazelnuts.

4 Divide the batter between the prepared tins and spread level. Bake in the oven for 1¼ hours. If the meringues brown too quickly, protect with a sheet of foil. Leave to stand for 5 minutes, then carefully run a palette knife (metal spatula) around the inside edge of the tins to loosen. Turn out on to a wire rack to cool.

5 For the filling, whip the cream until firm. Spread half the cream on one meringue and top with half the raspberries. Top with the other meringue. Spread the remaining cream on top and decorate with the remaining raspberries. Chill for about 1 hour to make cutting easier.

BLACK FOREST GATEAU

*A perfect gâteau for a special occasion tea party, or for serving as a
sumptuous dessert at a dinner party.*

INGREDIENTS

SERVES 10–12
5 size 3 eggs
*175 g/6 oz/¾ cup caster
(superfine) sugar*
*50 g/2 oz/½ cup plain (all-purpose)
flour, sifted*
50 g/2 oz/¾ cup cocoa powder, sifted
75 g/3 oz/6 tbsp butter, melted

FOR THE FILLING
5–6 tbsp Kirsch
*600 ml/1 pint/2½ cups double
(heavy) cream*
*425 g/15 oz can black cherries,
drained, stoned (pitted) and chopped*

TO DECORATE
*225 g/8 oz plain
(semi-sweet) chocolate*
*15–20 fresh cherries, preferably
with stems*
*sifted icing (confectioner's) sugar
(optional)*

1 Preheat the oven to 180°C/
350°F/Gas 4. Carefully grease
two deep 20 cm/8 inch round cake
tins, line both of the bases with
greaseproof (wax) paper and then
lightly grease the paper. Place the
eggs and caster (superfine) sugar in a
large mixing bowl and beat with an
electric mixer for about 10 minutes
or until the mixture is thick and pale
in colour.

3 Cut each cake horizontally in
half and sprinkle with the
Kirsch. In a large bowl, whip the
cream until it holds soft peaks.
Transfer two-thirds of the cream to
another bowl and stir in the chopped
cherries. Place a layer of cake on a
plate and spread over one-third of
the filling. Top with another layer of
cake and continue layering, finishing
with a layer of cake. Use the
remaining whipped cream to cover
the top and sides of the gâteau.

2 Sift together the plain
(all-purpose) flour and cocoa
powder, then sift again into the
whisked egg mixture. Fold in very
gently to retain as much air as
possible, then slowly trickle in the
melted butter and fold in gently.
Carefully divide the mixture between
the prepared tins. Bake in the centre
of the oven for about 30 minutes,
or until the tops of the cakes are
springy to the touch. Leave in the
tins for about 5 minutes, then
turn out on to a wire rack,
peel off the lining paper and leave
the cakes to cool completely.

4 To decorate the gâteau, melt the
chocolate in a bowl over a pan
of hot water. Spread the chocolate
out on to a plastic chopping board
and allow to set. Using a long sharp
knife, scrape along the surface of the
chocolate to make thin shavings and
use these to cover the sides and the
top of the cake. Arrange the cherries
on top of the gâteau. Dust with
icing (confectioner's) sugar, if wished.

LUXURY WHITE CHOCOLATE CHEESECAKE

*To ensure an even crust, use a dessertspoon or tablespoon to press the crumbs
on to the base and side of the tin.*

INGREDIENTS

SERVES 16–20
*150 g/5 oz (about 16–18) digestive
biscuits (graham crackers)
70 g/2½ oz/generous ½ cup blanched
hazelnuts, toasted
50 g/2 oz/4 tbsp unsalted (sweet)
butter, melted
½ tsp ground cinnamon*

FOR THE FILLING
*350 g/12 oz fine quality white
chocolate, chopped
120 ml/4 fl oz/½ cup whipping
or double (heavy) cream
675 g/1½ lb/3 cups cream cheese,
softened
50 g/2 oz/¼ cup granulated sugar
4 size 3 eggs
2 tbsp hazelnut-flavour liqueur or
1 tbsp vanilla essence (extract)*

FOR THE TOPPING
*425 ml/15 fl oz/1¾ cups sour cream
50 g/2 oz/¼ cup granulated sugar
1 tbsp hazelnut-flavour liqueur or
1 tsp vanilla essence (extract)
white chocolate curls to decorate
cocoa powder for dusting (optional)*

STORING
*Place in a covered container and keep
in the refrigerator for up to 2 days.*

1 Preheat the oven to 180°C/350°F/
Gas 4. Then carefully grease a 23
cm/9 inch springform tin, 7.5 cm/3
inch deep. Line the base with
greaseproof (wax) paper and grease
the paper. Process the biscuits
(crackers) and hazelnuts in a food
processor until fine crumbs form.
Pour in the butter and cinnamon.
Process just until blended. Using the
back of a spoon, press on to the base
and to within 1 cm/½ inch of the top
of the tin. Bake for 5–7 minutes, until
just set. Put the tin on a wire rack to
cool. Lower the oven temperature to
150°C/300°F/Gas 2.

2 To prepare the filling, in a small
saucepan over a low heat stir
together the white chocolate and
cream until smooth. Leave to cool. In
a large bowl beat the cream cheese
and sugar until smooth. Add the eggs
one at a time, beating well after each
addition. Slowly beat in the white
chocolate mixture and liqueur or
vanilla essence (extract). Pour into
the baked crust. Place the tin on a
baking (cookie) sheet. Bake for
45–55 minutes, or until the edge of
the cake is firm but the centre
slightly soft. Do not allow to
brown. Place on a wire rack.
Increase the oven temperature to
200°C/400°F/Gas 6.

3 To prepare the topping, in a small bowl whisk together the sour cream, sugar and liqueur or vanilla. Pour over the cheesecake, spreading evenly, and return to the oven. Bake for 5–7 minutes. Turn off the oven, but do not open the door for 1 hour.

4 Place the tin on a wire rack to cool to room temperature. Run a knife around the edge of the cake to separate it from the side; this helps prevent cracking. Cool then chill, loosely covered, overnight. To serve, remove the side of the springform tin. Place a large palette knife (metal spatula) between the base of the tin and the lining paper and slide the cake and paper base on to a serving plate. Decorate top of cake with chocolate curls and dust lightly with cocoa.

APRICOT BRANDY-SNAP ROULADE

*A magnificent combination of soft and crisp textures, this cake
looks impressive and is easy to prepare.*

INGREDIENTS

SERVES 6–8
4 size 3 eggs, separated
½ tbsp fresh orange juice
*115 g/4 oz/½ cup caster
(superfine) sugar*
175 g/6 oz/1½ cups ground almonds
*4 brandy snap biscuits (cookies),
crushed, to decorate*

FOR THE FILLING
150 g/5 oz can apricots, drained
*300 ml/½ pint/1¼ cups double
(heavy) cream*
*25 g/1 oz/4 tbsp icing (confectioner's)
sugar*

STORING
This cake is not suitable for storing.

1 Preheat the oven to 190°C/375°F/
Gas 5. Grease a 33 x 23 cm/
13 x 9 inch Swiss roll tin (jelly roll
pan), line with greaseproof (wax)
paper and grease the paper. Place the
egg yolks, orange juice and sugar in a
bowl and beat with an electric mixer
for 10 minutes until thick and pale.
Fold in the ground almonds.

2 Whisk the egg whites until they
hold stiff peaks and fold into the
almond mixture. Transfer to the
prepared tin and smooth the surface.
Bake in the centre of the oven for
about 20 minutes or until a skewer
inserted into the centre comes out
clean. Leave to cool in the tin,
covered with a clean, just-damp
dish towel.

3 To make the filling, purée the
apricots in a blender or food
processor. Place the cream and icing
(confectioner's) sugar in a mixing
bowl and whip until it holds soft
peaks. Fold in the apricot purée.

4 Spread out the crushed brandy
snaps on a sheet of greaseproof
paper. Spread about one-third of the
cream mixture over the cake, then
invert it on to the crushed brandy
snaps. Peel away the lining paper.
Use the remaining cream to cover the
cake. Using the greaseproof paper as
a guide, tightly roll up the roulade
from a short end. Transfer to a
serving dish, sticking on any
remaining pieces of brandy snaps.

Fresh Fruit Genoese

*This Italian classic, "Genovese con Panne e Frutta", can be made with
any type of soft fresh fruit.*

INGREDIENTS

SERVES 8–10
FOR THE SPONGE
*175 g/6 oz/1½ cups plain (all-purpose)
flour, sifted
pinch of salt
4 size 3 eggs
115 g/4 oz/½ cup caster
(superfine) sugar
6 tbsp orange-flavoured liqueur*

FOR THE FILLING AND TOPPING
*600 ml/1 pint/2½ cups double
(heavy) cream
4 tbsp vanilla sugar
450 g/1 lb fresh soft fruit, such as
raspberries, blueberries, cherries, etc.
150 g/5 oz/1¼ cups shelled pistachios,
finely chopped
4 tbsp apricot preserve, warmed and
sieved, to glaze*

STORING
This cake is not suitable for storing.

1 Preheat the oven to 180°C/350°F/
Gas 4. Grease a 21 cm/8½ inch
round springform cake tin, line the
base with greaseproof (wax) paper
and grease the paper. Sift the flour
and salt together three times, then set
aside. Place the eggs and sugar in a
mixing bowl and beat with an
electric mixer for about 10 minutes
or until thick and pale.

2 Sift the reserved flour mixture
into the mixing bowl, then fold
in very gently. Transfer the cake
mixture to the prepared tin. Bake in
the centre of the oven for 30–35
minutes or until a skewer inserted
into the centre of the cake comes out
clean. Leave the cake in the tin for
about 5 minutes, then turn out on to
a wire rack, peel off the lining paper
and leave to cool completely.

3 Cut the cake horizontally into
two layers, and place the base
layer on a serving plate. Sprinkle the
orange-flavoured liqueur over both
layers. Place the double (heavy)
cream and vanilla sugar in a mixing
bowl and beat with an electric mixer
until it holds soft peaks.

4 Spread two-thirds of the cream
over the base layer of cake and
top with half the fruit. Place the
second layer of cake on top and
spread the remaining cream over the
top and sides. Using a palette knife
(metal spatula), lightly press the
chopped nuts evenly around the
sides. Arrange the remaining fresh
fruit on top and brush lightly with
the apricot jam.

CHOCOLATE CAPPUCCINO CAKE

*If desired the cake can be left whole and rolled roulade-style, or baked in
2 x 23 cm/9 inch tins for a round cake.*

SERVES 8–10
175 g/6 oz plain (semi-sweet)
chocolate, chopped
2 tsp instant espresso powder
dissolved in 3 tbsp boiling water
6 size 3 eggs, separated
150 g/5 oz/¾ cup granulated sugar
pinch of cream of tartar
unsweetened cocoa powder, for sifting
chocolate-coated coffee beans,
to decorate

FOR THE COFFEE CREAM FILLING
175 ml/6 fl oz/¾ cup whipping cream
25 g/1 oz/2 tbsp granulated sugar
225 g/8 oz/1 cup mascarpone or cream
cheese, softened
2 tbsp coffee-flavoured liqueur
25 g/1 oz plain (semi-sweet) chocolate,
grated

FOR THE COFFEE BUTTERCREAM
4 egg yolks, at room temperature
70 ml/2½ fl oz/¾ cup light golden
syrup (corn syrup)
50 g/2 oz/¾ cup granulated sugar
225 g/8 oz/1 cup unsalted (sweet)
butter, diced and softened
1 tbsp instant espresso powder
dissolved in 1–2 tsp boiling water
15–30 ml/1–2 tbsp coffee-flavoured
liqueur

1 Preheat the oven to 180°C/350°F/
Gas 4. Grease a 40 x 27 cm/
15½ x 10½ inch baking (cookie)
sheet. Line with non-stick baking
paper (baking parchment), leaving a
5 cm/2 inch overhang on each narrow
end. Grease the paper. In a double
boiler, over a low heat, heat the
chocolate and coffee liquid until they
are melted and smooth, stirring
frequently. Set aside. In a bowl whisk
the egg yolks and sugar with an
electric mixer until thick and pale.
Gently stir in the chocolate mixture
until evenly blended.

2 In a large bowl beat the egg
whites and cream of tartar until
stiff. Stir a spoonful of whites into
the chocolate mixture to lighten it,
then fold in the rest. Pour the batter
into the prepared tin, spreading into
the corners. Bake for 12–15 minutes
until the top springs back when
touched lightly with a fingertip.
Sprinkle a clean dish towel with
cocoa powder, and then cover and
turn the cake out on to it. Peel off
the paper and cool.

3 To prepare the coffee cream
filling, whip the cream and
sugar in a large bowl until soft peaks
form. In another bowl, beat the
mascarpone or cream cheese and
coffee-flavoured liqueur until smooth.
Stir in the grated chocolate and fold
in the whipped cream. Cover and
chill until needed.

4 To prepare the buttercream, in a bowl with an electric mixer beat the yolks until thick and pale. In a saucepan over a medium heat, cook the syrup and sugar until boiling, stirring constantly. Slowly pour the hot syrup over the beaten yolks in a slow stream, beating continuously. Continue beating until the mixture is cool. Gradually beat in the butter until the mixture is smooth. Beat in the coffee and liqueur. Chill until thick enough to spread.

5 To assemble the cake, with a serrated knife, trim the edges of the cake. Cut the cake crossways into three equal strips. Place one cake strip on a plate and spread with half the coffee cream filling. Cover with a second cake strip and the remaining filling. Top with the remaining cake strip. Spoon about one-third of the coffee buttercream into a small piping bag fitted with a small star nozzle. Then spread the remaining buttercream on the top and sides of the cake. Pipe decoratively on the top and edges of the cake and decorate with chocolate-coated coffee beans.

STRAWBERRY CREAM GATEAU

Fresh raspberries also work well for this recipe.

INGREDIENTS

SERVES 8–10
2 egg yolks
4 size 3 eggs
finely grated rind of 1 lemon
115 g/4 oz/½ cup caster
(superfine) sugar
115 g/4 oz/1 cup plain (all-purpose)
flour, sifted
115 g/4 oz/½ cup butter, melted

FOR THE STRAWBERRY CREAM
225 g/8 oz/1½ cups fresh strawberries,
washed, dried and hulled
300 ml/½ pint/1¼ cups double (heavy)
cream
50 g/2 oz/½ cup icing (confectioner's)
sugar
1 tbsp strawberry liqueur or Kirsch

STORING
This cake can be kept for up to 2 days
in the refrigerator.

1 Preheat the oven to 150°C/300°F/ Gas 2. Grease a deep 20 cm/ 8 inch round cake tin, line the base with greaseproof (wax) paper and grease the paper. Place the egg yolks, eggs, lemon rind and sugar in a mixing bowl and beat with an electric mixer for about 10 minutes or until thick and pale. Add the flour and melted butter. Whisk for a further minute, then transfer to the prepared cake tin.

2 Bake in the centre of the oven for 30–35 minutes or until a skewer inserted into the centre of the cake comes out clean. Turn out on to a wire rack, peel off the lining paper and leave to cool completely.

3 To make the strawberry cream, place all but one of the strawberries in a food processor or blender and purée until smooth. Place the double (heavy) cream in a mixing bowl and whisk until it holds soft peaks. Fold the purée into the cream with the icing (confectioner's) sugar and liqueur or Kirsch.

4 Place the cooled cake on a plate and spread the strawberry cream evenly over the top and the sides, making swirls to create an attractive finish. Slice the reserved strawberry and use to decorate the cake top.

BAKED CHEESECAKE WITH FRESH FRUITS

*A rich, creamy cheesecake, baked on a sweet biscuit (graham cracker) base. It is topped
with a selection of exotic fresh fruits; vary the decoration to suit the season.*

INGREDIENTS

SERVES 12

*175 g/6 oz/1¼ cups crushed digestive
biscuits (graham crackers)*

*50 g/2 oz/¼ cup unsalted (sweet)
butter, melted*

*450 g/1 lb curd cheese (farmer's-style
cottage cheese)*

150 ml/¼ pint/⅔ cup sour cream

*115 g/4 oz/½ cup caster
(superfine) sugar*

3 size 3 eggs, separated

grated rind 1 lemon

2 tbsp Marsala

½ tsp almond essence (extract)

50 g/2 oz/½ cup ground almonds

*50 g/2 oz/scant ½ cup sultanas
(golden raisins)*

FOR THE TOPPING

*450 g/1 lb prepared mixed fruits – figs,
cherries, peaches, strawberries, hulled,
halved and stoned (pitted),
as necessary*

STORING

*This cake can be kept in the
refrigerator in an airtight container for
up to 3 days.*

1 Preheat the oven to 180°C/350°F/
Gas 4. Grease a 25 cm/10 inch
round springform tin. Line the side
of the tin with non-stick baking
paper (baking parchment).

3 Whisk the egg whites until stiff
and then fold into the creamed
mixture, with both the remaining
ingredients, until evenly combined.
Pour over the chilled biscuit base
(crust) and bake for 45 minutes, until
risen and just set in the centre.

2 Mix the biscuits (graham
crackers) with the butter until
well combined and press into the
base of the prepared tin. Smooth the
surface with a metal spoon and chill
for 20 minutes. Meanwhile prepare
the cake mixture. Beat the cheese,
cream, sugar, egg yolks, lemon rind,
Marsala and almond essence (extract)
together until smooth and creamy.

4 Remove from the oven and leave
in the tin in a warm, draught-
free place, until completely cold.
Remove the side of the tin and peel
off the lining paper. Chill for 1 hour
before decorating with the prepared
fruits, just before serving.

Simnel Cake

A traditional cake for Easter.

3 Bake in the centre of the oven for about 2½ hours or until golden and springy to the touch. Leave the cake in the tin for about 15 minutes, then turn out on to a wire rack, peel off the lining paper and leave to cool completely.

1 Preheat the oven to 160°C/325°F/ Gas 3. Lightly grease a deep 20 cm/8 inch round cake tin, then carefully line with a double thickness of greaseproof (wax) paper and grease the paper. Place the softened butter and caster (superfine) sugar in a bowl and beat with an electric mixer until light and fluffy. Gradually beat in the eggs, beating well after each addition. Stir in the dried fruit, glacé (candied) cherries and sherry, if using. Sift together the plain (all-purpose) flour, mixed spice (apple pie spice) and baking powder, then fold into the cake mixture. Set aside until needed.

2 Cut off half of the marzipan and roll it out on a work surface that has been lightly dusted with icing (confectioner's) sugar to a round measuring 20 cm/8 inch. Spoon half of the cake mixture into the prepared tin and smooth the surface with the back of a spoon. Place the marzipan round on top, then add the other half of the cake mixture and smooth the surface.

4 Roll out the other half of the marzipan to a round to fit on top of the cake. Brush the top of the cake with the jam and position the marzipan on top. Flute the edges of the marzipan and make a decorative pattern on top with a fork. Brush with egg yolk. Put the cake on a baking (cookie) sheet and place under a grill (broiler) for 5 minutes or until the top is lightly browned. Leave the cake to cool completely before decorating with ribbons and sugared eggs.

NUT AND CANDIED FRUIT RING

*The cake can be made 2–3 weeks before Christmas. Store it
in a tin in a cool place until needed.*

INGREDIENTS

SERVES 10–12

115 g/4 oz/½ cup glacé (candied)
cherries, quartered
115 g/4 oz/generous ¾ cup raisins or
sultanas (golden raisins)
115 g/4 oz/½ cup dried apricots,
quartered
115 g/4 oz dried prunes, stoned
(pitted) and quartered
115 g/4 oz/⅔ cup stoned (pitted) and
chopped dates
4 tbsp rum, brandy or sherry
115 g/4 oz/½ cup butter
115 g/4 oz/½ cup soft dark brown
sugar
½ tsp ground cinnamon
½ tsp mixed spice
(apple pie spice)
2 size 3 eggs, beaten
50 g/2 oz/½ cup ground almonds
115 g/4 oz/1 cup coarsely chopped
walnuts
225 g/8 oz/2 cups self-raising flour

FOR THE TOPPING
2 tbsp rum, brandy or sherry
4 tbsp apricot jam
whole blanched almonds, split
3 glacé (candied) cherries, halved
a few strips of angelica

STORING
*This cake will keep for 2–3 weeks in
an airtight container.*

1 The day before you bake the
cake, soak all the dried fruit in
the rum, brandy or sherry. Cover
and leave overnight. Grease a 23 cm/
9 inch ring tin (ring mold), with a
1.5 litre/2½ pint/6¼ cup capacity.

3 Spoon the mixture into the
prepared cake tin, level the top
and bake for 1½– 2 hours or until a
skewer inserted into the centre comes
out clean. Leave to cool in the tin
for 30 minutes then turn out on to a
wire rack to cool completely. Brush
with the rum, brandy or sherry.

2 Preheat the oven to 160°C/325°F/
Gas 3. In a bowl, beat the butter,
sugar and spices together until light
and fluffy. Beat in the eggs, and fold
in the soaked fruits. Mix in the
almonds, walnuts and flour.

4 Gently heat the apricot jam in a
small pan. Sieve (strain) the jam.
Brush the glaze over the top of the
cake. Decorate with the nuts and
fruit and brush them liberally with
more apricot glaze, which must be
hot, or the decoration will lift off
while you are brushing on the jam.

MOIST AND RICH CHRISTMAS CAKE

The cake can be made 4–6 weeks before Christmas. During this time,
pierce the cake with a fine skewer and spoon over 2–3 tbsp brandy.

INGREDIENTS

MAKES 1 CAKE

225 g/8 oz/generous 1½ cups sultanas
(golden raisins)
225 g/8 oz/1 cup currants
225 g/8 oz/generous 1½ cups raisins
115 g/4 oz dried prunes, stoned
(pitted) and chopped
50 g/2 oz glacé (candied) cherries,
halved
50 g/2 oz/¾ cup mixed (candied) peel,
chopped
3 tbsp brandy or sherry
225 g/8 oz/2 cups plain (all-purpose)
flour
pinch of salt
½ tsp ground cinnamon
½ tsp grated nutmeg
1 tbsp cocoa powder
225 g/8 oz/1 cup butter
225 g/8 oz/1 generous cup soft dark
brown sugar
4 size 1 eggs
finely grated rind of 1 orange or
lemon
50 g/2 oz/½ cup ground almonds
50 g/2 oz/½ cup chopped almonds

TO DECORATE

4 tbsp apricot jam
25 cm/10 in round cake board
450 g/1 lb marzipan
450 g/1 lb white fondant icing
225 g/8 oz royal icing
1.5 m/1½ yd ribbon

1 The day before baking the cake, put all the fruit to soak in the brandy or sherry. Cover and leave overnight. Grease a 20 cm/8 inch deep round cake tin and line it with a double thickness of greaseproof (wax) paper.

2 The next day, preheat the oven to 160°C/325°F/Gas 3. Sift together the flour, salt, spices and cocoa powder. Beat the butter and sugar together until light and fluffy and beat in the eggs gradually. Mix in the orange or lemon rind, the ground and chopped almonds, dried fruits (with any liquid) and the flour mixture. Spoon into the prepared cake tin and level the top. Bake for 3 hours, or until a skewer inserted into the centre comes out clean.

3 Transfer the cake tin to a wire rack and leave to cool for an hour. Carefully turn the cake out on to the wire rack, but leave the paper on if the cake is to be stored, as it will help to keep it moist. Warm then sieve (strain) the apricot jam to make a glaze. Remove the paper from the cake, place on a cake board and brush with apricot glaze. Cover the cake with marzipan and then fondant icing. Pipe a border around the base of the cake with royal icing. Tie a ribbon around the sides. Roll out any fondant icing trimmings and stamp out 12 small holly leaves with a cutter. Make one bell motif with a biscuit cutter, dusted first with sifted icing (confectioner's) sugar. Roll 36 small balls for the holly berries. Leave on greaseproof (wax) paper to dry for 24 hours. Then use to decorate the cake attaching them with a little royal icing.

PASSION CAKE

The icing thickens quickly as it cools and will become difficult to spread, so have the cake on a serving plate and a palette knife (metal spatula) ready to spread the icing.

INGREDIENTS

SERVES 8
150 g/5 oz/⅔ cup butter
200 g/7 oz/scant 1 cup soft light
brown sugar
2 size 3 eggs, beaten
175 g/6 oz carrots, finely grated
finely grated rind of 1 orange
large pinch of salt
1 tsp ground cinnamon
½ tsp grated nutmeg
200 g/7 oz/1¼ cups self-raising flour
1 tsp baking powder
115 g/4 oz/generous ¾ cup raisins
50 g/2 oz/½ cup chopped walnuts
2 tbsp milk

FOR THE ICING
450 g/1 lb/2¼ cups granulated sugar
150 ml/¼ pint/⅔ cup water
pinch of cream of tartar
2 egg whites

STORING
*This cake will keep for up to 4 days,
covered, in a cool place.*

1 Preheat the oven to 190°C/375°F/ Gas 5. Grease two 20 cm/8 inch sandwich tins, then line the bases with greaseproof (wax) paper and grease the paper.

2 In a bowl, beat together the butter and sugar until pale and fluffy. Beat in the eggs gradually and then stir in all the remaining ingredients to make a mixture with a soft dropping consistency.

3 Spoon the mixture into the prepared cake tins and bake for 25–30 minutes, or until the cakes are firm to the touch. Leave the cakes to cool in the tins for 5 minutes. Then turn out on to a wire rack and leave to cool completely.

4 For the icing, put the sugar and water in a pan and heat very gently to dissolve the sugar. (Swirl the pan to mix the sugar, do not stir it with a spoon.) Add the cream of tartar and bring to the boil. Boil until the syrup reaches 115°C/240°F on a sugar thermometer or the soft ball stage. Quickly dip the base of the pan in cold water. Whisk the egg whites until they are stiff and pour the syrup on to them, whisking all the time. Continue whisking until the icing loses its satiny appearance and holds its shape. Quickly sandwich the cakes with some of the icing and spread the rest over the top and side of the cake.

CHOCOLATE CHRISTMAS LOG

Begin preparations for this cake at least 1 day ahead as although it is easy to prepare it has several components.

INGREDIENTS

SERVES 12–14

5 size 3 eggs, separated

20 g/³⁄₄ oz/3 tbsp unsweetened cocoa powder, plus extra for dusting

115 g/4 oz/1 cup icing (confectioner's) sugar

³⁄₄ tsp cream of tartar

FOR THE CHOCOLATE GANACHE FROSTING

300 ml/¹⁄₂ pint/1¹⁄₄ cups double (heavy) or whipping cream

350 g/12 oz bittersweet chocolate, chopped

2 tbsp brandy or chocolate-flavour liqueur

FOR THE CRANBERRY SAUCE

450 g/1 lb fresh or frozen cranberries, rinsed and picked over

280 g/10 oz/1 cup seedless raspberry preserve, melted

90 g/3¹⁄₂ oz/¹⁄₂ cup granulated sugar, or to taste

FOR THE WHITE CHOCOLATE CREAM FILLING

200 g/7 oz fine quality white chocolate, chopped

475 ml/16 fl oz/2 cups double (heavy) cream

2 tbsp brandy or chocolate-flavour liqueur (optional)

1 To make the ganache frosting, in a saucepan over a medium heat, bring the cream to the boil. Remove from the heat and add the chocolate all at once, stirring constantly until smooth. Stir in the liqueur, if using, then strain into a bowl and cool. Chill until needed.

3 For the cake, preheat the oven to 200°C/400°F/Gas 6. Grease a 39 x 26 cm/15¹⁄₂ x 10¹⁄₂ inch Swiss roll tin (jelly roll pan), line with non-stick baking paper (baking parchment), overlapping the edge by 2.5 cm/1 inch. Whisk the egg yolks until thick and creamy. Whisk in the cocoa and half the sugar. In a large bowl whisk the egg whites until frothy. Add the cream of tartar and whisk until soft peaks form. Add the remaining sugar, 2 tbsp at a time, whisking well after each addition, until stiff and glossy. Fold the yolk mixture into the whites.

2 To make the sauce, in a food processor, process the cranberries until liquid. Press through a sieve (strainer) into a bowl, discarding the pulp. Stir in the raspberry preserve and sugar to taste. If sauce is too thick, add a little water.

4 Spread the batter in the prepared tin and bake for 15–20 minutes. Lay a clean dish towel on a work surface and cover with non-stick baking paper; dust with cocoa or sugar. Immediately turn the cake out on to the paper. Peel off the lining paper. Trim the edges and, starting from one narrow end, roll up the cake together with the paper and towel. Leave to cool.

5 To make the filling, in a
saucepan gently heat the white
chocolate with 120 ml/4 fl oz/½ cup
cream until melted, stirring frequently.
Strain into a bowl and cool. Whisk
the remaining cream and brandy until
soft peaks form. Stir a spoonful of
cream into the white chocolate
mixture to lighten it, then fold in
remaining cream. Unroll the cake and
spread with chocolate cream. Starting
from the same end, re-roll the cake
without the paper. Cut off one-quarter
at an angle. Place against the long
piece to resemble a branch.

6 Allow the frosting to soften at
room temperature. With an
electric mixer, beat the ganache until
light in colour and texture, about
30–45 seconds. It should be a soft
spreading consistency; do not over-
beat as it will become stiff and
grainy. Using a palette knife (metal
spatula), spread the ganache over the
cake. Using a fork, mark to resemble
tree bark. Then dust with icing
(confectioner's) sugar and serve with
the cranberry sauce.

PANFORTE

This rich, spicy nougat-type cake is a speciality of Siena in Italy,
where it is traditionally baked at Christmas.

INGREDIENTS

SERVES 8

280 g/10 oz/2 cups mixed (candied)
exotic peel, to include: papaya,
pineapple, orange, lemon and citron
115 g/4 oz/1 cup unblanched almonds
50 g/2 oz/½ cup walnut halves
50 g/2 oz/½ cup plain
(all-purpose) flour
1 tsp ground cinnamon
¼ tsp each grated nutmeg, ground
cloves and ground coriander
175 g/6 oz/¾ cup caster (superfine)
sugar
4 tbsp water
icing (confectioner's) sugar,
to decorate

STORING

This cake will keep well for several
weeks in an airtight container.

1 Preheat the oven to 180°C/350°F/
Gas 4. Grease a 20 cm/8 inch
round loose-based tin and line the
base with a circle of rice paper.
Combine the mixed (candied) peel
and almonds and walnuts in a bowl.
Sift in the flour and all the spices
and mix well. Heat the sugar and
water in a small pan, stirring until
the sugar is completely dissolved.
Increase the heat and boil until the
mixture reaches 115°C/220°F on a
sugar thermometer, or until it reaches
the thread stage.

2 Remove from the heat and pour
on to the fruit mixture, stirring
with a wooden spoon until well-
coated. Transfer to the prepared tin,
pressing out with the back of a metal
spoon. Bake in the centre of the oven
for 25–30 minutes, until the mixture
is bubbling. Remove from the oven
and cool in the tin for 5 minutes.

3 With a lightly oiled palette knife
(metal spatula) work around the
edge of the cake, to loosen and
remove from the tin leaving the base
in place. Leave until cold.

4 Remove the panforte from
the base and decorate with a
generous dusting of icing
(confectioner's) sugar.

INDEX